The dark will hide here

By: H.N Williams

A Warning Before You Enter:

Within these pages, the shadows speak and the light stirs quietly.

Here you will find sorrow, survival, loss, and the fierce beating heart of hope.

*Tread softly, dear reader.
Some paths may ache.
Some truths may burn.*

But know: even in the deepest woods, the smallest light still leads the way.

I looked the devil in the face and called him love.
I saw his dead black heart and thought there were flowers somewhere in the cracks.
Between every word he said to break me, I convinced myself I could save him.
Every time he put his cold, dead hands around my neck, I convinced myself it would not be this way forever

I let him put out pieces of the light that burned in my soul.
Little by little, I was fading away.
Until he thought he had smothered me — nothing left but a shell
where a kind, hopeless dreamer once lived

*But he did not know
he was toying with a fighter,
a survivor.
I took the last speck of light in me
and hid it deep within the aching depths of
my chest.
Until one day,
it was ready to engulf me once more.*

The fire exploded in my chest.
The anger and rage at what I had become —
what I had let him do to me —
fueled the flames.
That was when I decided:
I would never let him talk to me like that again.
I would never let him touch me again.

I let every memory of him that I once mistook for love burn.
I let the devil appear before me —
and I did not flinch.
He watched as I let the girl I used to be burn and die,
leaving behind only a scorched skeleton of her old ways

*No more feelings of false hope for a false lover.
No more mistaking my softness for weakness.
No one would stomp on my flames again without getting burned.
Only those who will fan the fire
will feel the love I have to offer*

I am not your victim
I did EVERYTHING for you to keep you afloat.
Any more, and I would have given the skin off my back.
I let you embarrass me.
You stole from my family who gave you a home when your own family abandoned you. I helped you and your mom through chemo,
Gave you countless money, let you say terrible things about me.

*You held a knife to my throat.
It plays over and over again in my head.
You took a gun and threatened to shoot yourself.
I had to take the gun from you.
I gave you my heart and soul because God
—
I just wanted you to get better.
I just wanted you to be happy.*

*You said you owed me your life and that I saved you —
but what you really meant was:
You are mine to destroy now.
You tried.
You tried so hard to destroy me.
Thank you for thinking the silent treatment would work on me.
Because I had already started to hate you before that.*

*I learned how to manipulate you back.
But when you were gone,
I felt peace for the first time in three years.
When you called again,
I felt a fire explode inside me.
No longer afraid.
I knew I was done.
I never wanted to hear your voice again,
never wanted to see you again.
I yelled at you at the top of my lungs:
I AM DONE WITH YOU.
It exhilarated me —
how speechless you were.*

*I see the messages you still send me —
even years later,
as I block every account.
I know I left you homeless with nothing.
I don't care anymore.
I am glad you are.
Maybe you will finally take care of yourself.
You should be locked up.*

I found out what you did to those other girls.
You disgust me.
I trusted you,
loved you,
believed in you.
You did not deserve it.
You know now how much you underestimated me.
If you ever show up here again —
you won't make it out alive.
I WILL NOT BE YOUR VICTIM.
I AM A SURVIVOR.

The scars you left on my mind may be here —
but I am not broken.
The grave you were digging for me —
I have climbed out of it.
You will never put another hand on me again.
And I hope you don't forget me:
The one who tried harder than anyone else ever would.
The one you tried to destroy —
but couldn't.
So you are left with nothing.
And no one.

Not everything is so black and white

*When you have to choose
to break your own bad cycles
to learn to choose to love yourself again.
You worked so hard to save him,
but he couldn't let his demons go.*

*You get tired of trying so hard
to just have the demons still show.
You held him as he wept,
and you made him laugh a million times.
You saw all he could be in those little
moments.
But you couldn't take the demons' threats,
and you couldn't shake the fear
of being struck upon once more.*

*One of the hardest things you can do
is leave a broken soul alone
to save yourself —
when you chose, for so long,
to love them more than yourself.
When you have saved their life so many
times
and told them you loved them
every single time —
even in their darkest times.*

*Leaving is so hard.
Not everything is so black and white.*

Silent battles

Trying my hardest to defeat my own demons.
They whisper mean things in silence.
They play horrendous scenes that terrify me,
over and over in my head.
I know they were left from the monsters I walked next to,
and thought it was love.
I tiptoe quietly through life —
it's how I have been forced to be,
when all I want to do is run and scream.

No value in love.
No value in life.
Lost hope.
Too much pride.
Every hit, scratch, and scream
is the torture trying to be released.
I'm trying to be brave and face my fears
even when I am afraid,
and I keep going
because I want to make it.
But the sinking in my stomach,
the heaviness in my chest,
is breaking me apart.

*If only they knew
the many times I have toyed with the idea
of giving it all up —
but it wouldn't matter
unless I was dead.
Go ahead, remind me of my demons.
You think I don't know them?
They lay upon me at night
until I am too exhausted,
and I fall asleep.*

*Do not mistake me for weak.
I have walked with demons
and did not fall to their ways.
I have a spark in my soul
that will always refuse to give up.*

I am sorry

*I wish I could tell my body sorry
for all the trauma that it's been through.
But just like when you tell someone sorry
and it's too late —
it's hard to forgive and let go.
I can feel its hurt
through every bone,
through every muscle,
unable to let go.*

*It manifests its suffering
through every ache,
every break,
every crack of my body.
With no end in sight.*

*So I can either give in and give up —
or keep fighting
through every ache and pain,
even when I feel like I am breaking.*

*I am sorry
I didn't love you in time.*

*Steady love
I used to want a crazy love,
made of explosions of excitement.
Now I just want a steady love,
a trusting love,
something that makes me feel safe
even on my hardest days.*

*It won't be like this forever
Some days
the only way to survive
is telling yourself
it won't be like this forever.*

Flash backs
It's been years,
and sometimes still,
in the silence of my thoughts,
I find myself back there.
I see the devil in your eyes.
I feel your claws around my neck.
Will these flashbacks ever go away?

Part of your survival
Playing victim is easy.
Blaming others is easy.
Letting that mentality keep you down is easy.

*Truly seeing yourself
and accepting it, flaws and all, is hard.
To see your mistakes
and say this is not my ending is hard.
To hold yourself accountable is not easy.
It's even harder to pick yourself back up
and put the pieces back together.
To do better.
Break bad habits.
Practice the good ones over and over
again.
To discipline yourself.
But this is part of your survival.
Don't let them win.*

Dressed in sweet lies
Evil is always dressed up
in fake good intentions
and lying words
that sound so sweet.

*Don't give up on yourself
The secret of doing big things
that people need to talk about more:
it's gonna hurt,
it's going to feel impossible.
They don't want you to know
how many times they gave up
and started again,
how many mistakes they made,
that you are probably gonna hate
a lot of the process
and still do it alone anyways.*

*Improvement is not some miracle.
It's work.
But you are gonna choose it.
You have to.
You are gonna take ten steps forward
and five steps back.
Up and down.*

*You are gonna be in pain.
You are gonna be tired.
It will feel never-ending.
You are going to toy with the idea of settling.
But you have to feed that voice in you that keeps you going,
that started you in this journey
in the first place,
the voice that saved you from the worst.*

Take a moment to scream.
Take a moment to cry.
Take a moment to sleep if you must.
But don't give up on yourself.

*Stop abandoning yourself
to please people.
To fit in with people.*

The theme of my life
Be the light,
stick to what you know is right.
Even when it feels like
the whole world is going left,
you know what you have to do.
Don't let go.
Don't ease up.
This has been the theme of my life.

Different skins
I have seen the same person,
just in different skins.
It's like they recognize me
and like to play pretend,
until they can't hide
the demon that lives within.
I used to think it was my job
to save them.
But now it just feels like
they were sent to smother me
and the light I have within.

Ink upon my skin
I wear this ink upon my skin
to show a warrior that lays within.
It tells my story in little ways
that I know no one knows how to read.

*But I am okay with that.
It shows my strength,
that the phases you go through are okay,
and to just keep going,
and that I am a survivor.
I have one piece that is very special to me,
that has become my biggest strength,
and how I know, no matter what,
I will never, ever give up.*

The never ending ditch
Depression feels like a deep ditch
that you can't climb out of.
You try and you try,
but it just keeps getting deeper
the more you try.
There are days,
and weeks,
even months,
it feels easier to just lie in the ditch
and become numb.
But that's not fair to you
and all you have done
to survive this far.

My biggest hope
I can blame myself,
and I can hate myself,
for letting another person
take advantage of my light.
But with that mistake,
God decided to bless me
with the greatest gift.
My biggest reason to be
the best I can be.
My biggest reason to keep going.
Because there are times
I feel like I don't love myself enough
to keep on living.
He gave me a little girl
that will forever be
my biggest strength —
to make sure she is happy and safe.
She is hope.

Underestimated
I will forever have ingrained in me
the anger I felt
when he put my little girl
in the way of his evil temper.
Only a few weeks old,
and he thought I was weak —
too weak to fight back,
to leave.

*But people love
to underestimate me.
I've learned
to like that about people.*

*My reason
When I look at her
and think about her,
I feel a warmth in me
that I didn't know existed anymore.
She has taught me
what truly loving someone feels like.
To give meaning to my fight,
when it felt so pointless before —
like it was just something
I had to do
for the sake of doing it.
But with her,
I know every reason
why I must do
what I must do.*

*She won't be afraid
I know if it's the last thing I ever do,
I will protect her and her little heart.
She won't know
the pain I have felt from you.
You think you are so scary,
but I have seen
and laid with
more fearsome monsters than you.
You are not clever.
You are not scary.
And the world doesn't revolve around you.
She won't be afraid of you.
And I will make sure of that.*

*Fire heart
I already see
the fearsome little fire heart
that lays within her.
I will let it grow,
and she will know
she is capable,
she is worthy,
and she is strong.*

*She will know,
when she runs into monsters,
that she will not need
a knight to slay them.
That she can save herself.*

*She won't need you
to feel loved
and worthy.*

I would like to add a few bonus poems that I wrote for my grandma who was a big part of my life. She passed away a few years ago.

To my grandma:
I am sorry I was so lost the last few years of your life.
That will always be one of my biggest regrets.
As I was fighting my way back to myself, I was wasting precious time with you.
But you were always my saving grace.

Some of my favorite memories growing up were with you during the summer days at your house.
I miss your voice most of all.
You made me feel capable,
even when I felt like I could never do anything right.
You were so strong and brave and kind and smart.

I wish you could have met your great-granddaughter.
But a part of me feels like you helped God pick her just for me.
I want to share a few poems I made for you.

*So far away
My soul still can't fathom
the idea of yours
being so far away.
But that's okay.
I knew
that I was going to miss you deeply,
and that I would never
stop.
From the time
that I was old enough
to know what death was,
I knew I was going to suffer deeply
when you left me here on earth.*

*My angel went to heaven
My angel went to heaven.
I prayed for the first time
in many years
the night before.
I am not sure what that means.
But the day you left,
the heavens cried for us,
and the day we had to say goodbye
at your funeral,
they cried for us some more.*

*Yes, my angel went home to heaven,
and somehow,
I have to figure out
how to live on earth
without her.*

Part of my Survival
My angel saved me
in more ways
than she will ever know.
I might have been dead
without her.
You were a part
of my survival story.

The saving voice
No matter what I did,
you always saw the good in me.
You always saw me
as the best parts of me,
even with the bad lingering there.

*That love kept me alive.
Your encouraging voice
became the voice
that told the demons in my head
to be quiet.
When all the bad thoughts
and anxiety would arise,
I would think of you
and how you thought of me.
I knew I had to prove to you
I was all those wonderful things
you saw in me.*

*One day
One day,
I will climb to the biggest mountain I can,
and at the top, I will scream.
I will scream for all the loss,
the battles,
the wins,
the heartache.
And most of all,
I will scream for you,
and I will scream for me.
And it will be wonderful
and freeing.
And maybe,
I will live
a little bit lighter
after that.*

*A letter to myself
I forgive you
for who you were,
and do not hate it,
because her innocence
was so beautiful.
That beautiful-hearted dreamer,
so naive and pure.*

*It's not your fault
for believing in snakes
disguised as good intentions.
You were so innocent
and did not know
how to guard your heart,
because your heart
did not know the world
was filled with such deception.
But it will all be okay,
and you will keep this light
in your heart alive,
despite all of it.*

Authors words to you :
This book was not written for perfection.
It was written for survival —
and for light.
For the moments when you are breaking,
and the moments when you are putting yourself
back together again.
If you find yourself between the lines of these pages,
know that you are not alone.
Know that your pain has been seen,
that your heart is understood,
and that even in your darkest hours,
your light has never stopped burning.

*You are not here to stay small,
to stay silent,
or to be swallowed by the shadows.
You are here to rise,
to break,
to rebuild,
and to shine —
with the kind of fierce, quiet light
only survivors can carry.
So take what you need from these words,
leave what you don't,
and remember:
you are allowed to be both
a masterpiece
and a work in progress,
both scarred
and luminous,
both survivor
and light-bearer.*

About the Author
H.N. Williams is a survivor, a mother, a dreamer, and a writer
who believes in the power of words to heal.
Her poetry is woven from the threads of survival and love,
of heartbreak and hope,
of loss and light.
Writing became her way back to herself —
a quiet rebellion against the pain,
and a soft place to land when the world felt heavy.
When she is not writing,
she finds joy in the small, ordinary moments:
the laughter of her daughter,
the memory of her grandmother's love,
and the unshakable belief
that even in the hardest seasons,
there is always a light
worth chasing.

Made in the USA
Coppell, TX
10 May 2025

49100317R00042